INTERNATIONAL SONGS FOR ~~Easy Guitar~~

E-Z GUITAR

WITH NOTES AND TAB

2 STRUM AND PICK PATTERNS

3 ACH DU LIEBER AUGUSTIN
Germany

4 ALOUETTE
France

6 ANNIE LAURIE
Scotland

8 AU CLAIR DE LA LUNE
France

10 AULD LANG SYNE
Scotland

12 AY! LINDA AMIGA
South America

14 ON THE BEAUTIFUL BLUE DANUBE, OP. 314
Austria

16 CAMPBELLS ARE COMING
Scotland

11 CARNIVAL OF VENICE
Italy

18 CHIAPANECAS
Mexico

20 CIELITO LINDO
Mexico

22 COME BACK TO SORRENTO
Italy

24 COMIN' THROUGH THE RYE
Scotland

26 DANNY BOY (LONDONDERRY AIR)
Ireland

25 DARK EYES
Russia

28 DU DU LIEGST MIR IM HERZEN
Germany

30 FUNICULI, FUNICULA
Italy

32 GREENSLEEVES
England

34 HAVA NAGILAH
Israel

33 JOHN PEEL
England

36 KUM BA YAH
Nigeria

38 LA CUCARACHA
Mexico

37 LA DONNA È MOBILE
Italy

40 LOCH LOMAND
Scotland

42 MARIANNE
Jamaica

44 MEXICAN HAT DANCE
Mexico

46 MOLLY MALONE (COCKLES & MUSSELS)
Ireland

48 MY BONNIE
Scotland

50 MY WILD IRISH ROSE
Ireland

54 'O SOLE MIO
Italy

53 PLAISIR D'AMOUR
France

56 SAKURA
Japan

64 SANTA LUCIA
Italy

58 TOOM BALALAIKA
Russia

60 VOLGA BOAT SONG
Russia

62 WHEN IRISH EYES ARE SMILING
Ireland

ISBN 0-7935-6953-2

HAL•LEONARD®
CORPORATION

7777 W. BLUEMOUND RD. P.O. BOX 13819 MILWAUKEE, WI 53213

Visit Hal Leonard Online at
www.halleonard.com

STRUM AND PICK PATTERNS

This chart contains the suggested strum and pick patterns that are referred to by number at the beginning
of each song in this book. The symbols ⊓ and ⌄ in the strum patterns refer to down and up strokes, respectively.
The letters in the pick patterns indicate which right-hand fingers plays which strings.

p = thumb
i = index finger
m = middle finger
a = ring finger

For example; Pick Pattern 2
is played: thumb - index - middle - ring

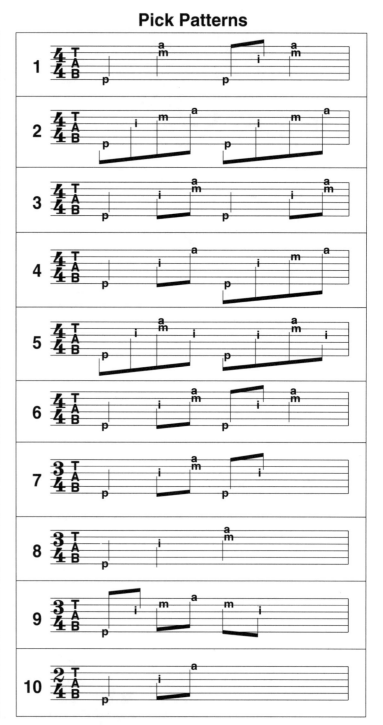

Strum Patterns   ## Pick Patterns

You can use the 3/4 Strum or Pick Patterns in songs written in compound meter (6/8, 9/8, 12/8, etc.).
For example, you can accompany a song in 6/8 by playing the 3/4 pattern twice in each measure.
The 4/4 Strum and Pick Patterns can be used for songs written in cut time (¢) by doubling the note
time values in the patterns. Each pattern would therefore last two measures in cut time.

Ach, Du Lieber Augustin

Traditional

Strum Pattern: 8, 9
Pick Pattern: 8

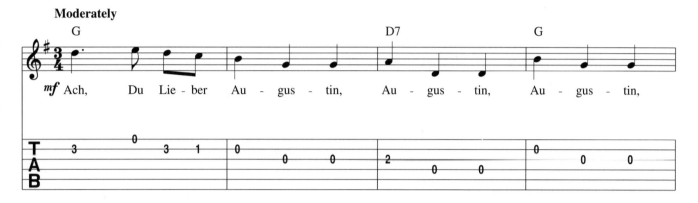

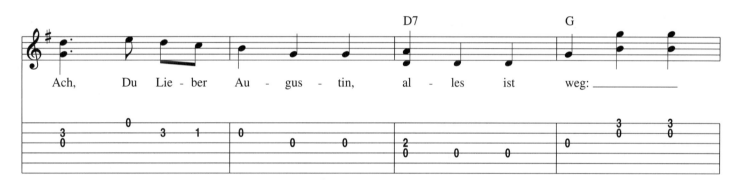

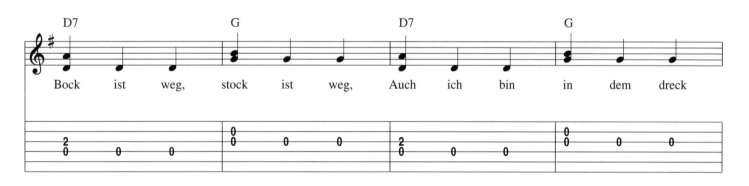

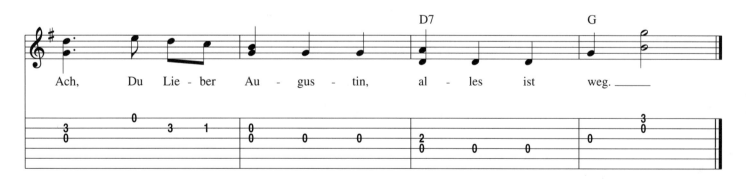

Alouette

Traditional

Strum Pattern: 10
Pick Pattern: 10

Chorus
Moderately

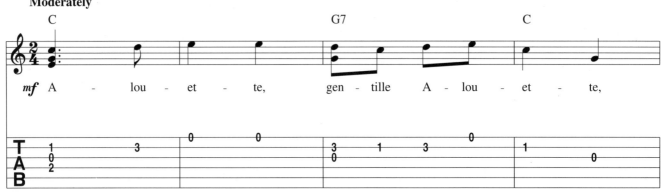

mf A - lou - et - te, gen - tille A - lou - et - te,

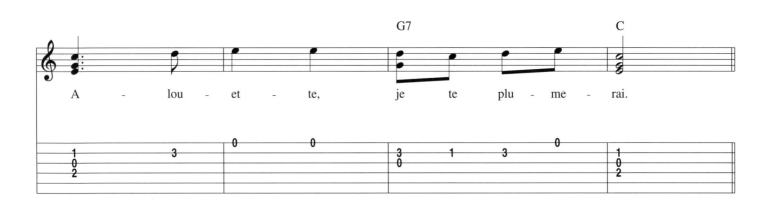

A - lou - et - te, je te plu - me - rai.

Verse

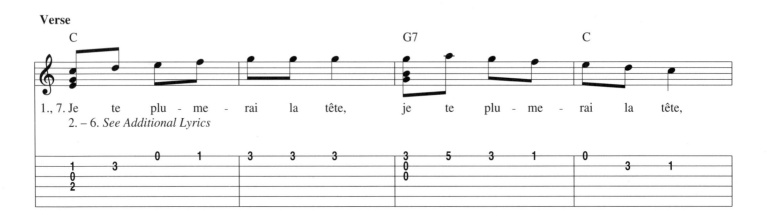

1., 7. Je te plu - me - rai la tête, je te plu - me - rai la tête,
2. – 6. *See Additional Lyrics*

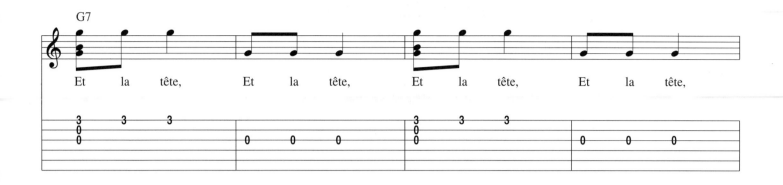

Et la tête, Et la tête, Et la tête, Et la tête,

play 7 times

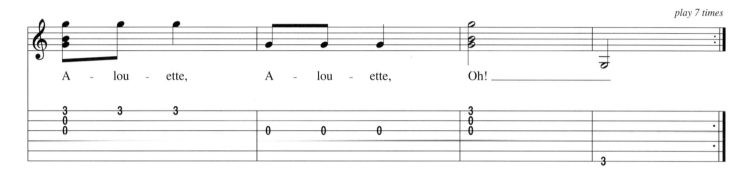

A - lou - ette, A - lou - ette, Oh! _____

Outro-Chorus

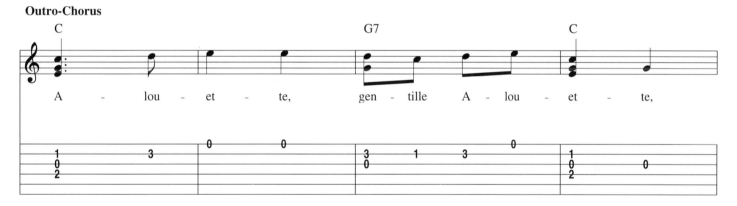

A - lou - et - te, gen - tille A - lou - et - te,

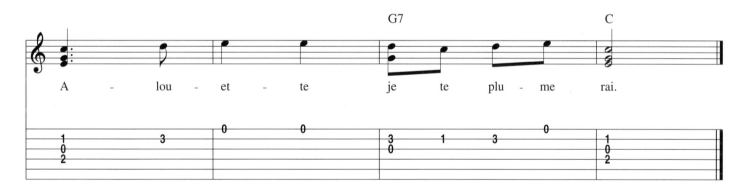

A - lou - et - te je te plu - me rai.

Additional Lyrics

2) le bec
3) le cou
4) les jambes
5) les pieds
6) les pattes

Annie Laurie

Traditional

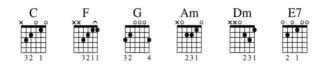

Strum Pattern: 5
Pick Pattern: 6

Verse

Slowly

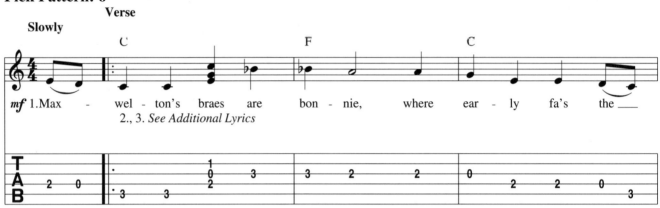

mf 1.Max - wel - ton's braes are bon - nie, where ear - ly fa's the ___
2., 3. *See Additional Lyrics*

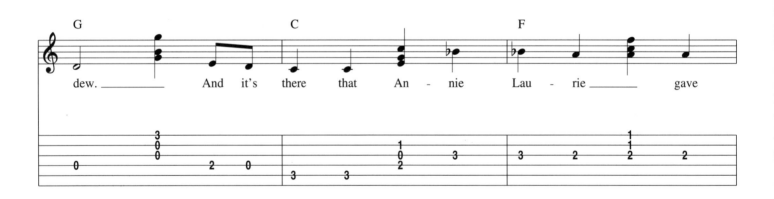

dew. ___ And it's there that An - nie Lau - rie ___ gave

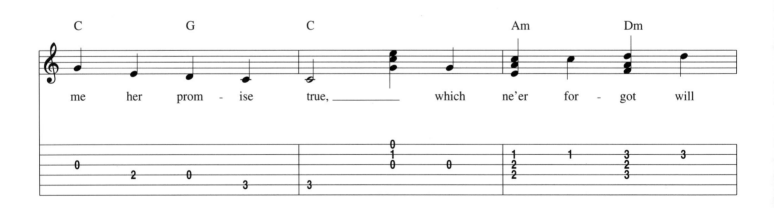

me her prom - ise true, ___ which ne'er for - got will

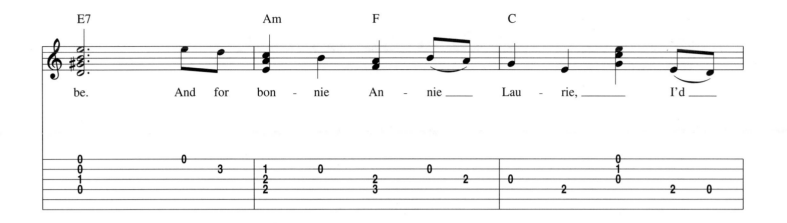

be. And for bon - nie An - nie ____ Lau - rie, _____ I'd ____

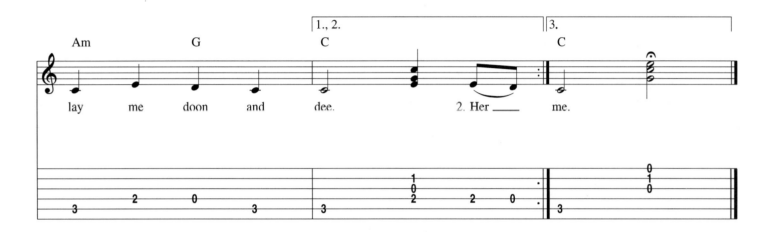

lay me doon and dee. 2. Her ____ me.

Additional Lyrics

2. Her brow is like the snawdrift,
   Her neck is like the swan,
   Her face it is the fairest
   That e'er the sun shone on,
   That e'er the sun shone on,
   An' dark blue is her ee.

3. Like dew on the gowan lying
   Is the fa' o' her fairy feet;
   An' like the winds in summer sighing,
   Her voice is low an' sweet,
   Her voice is low an' sweet,
   An' she's a' the world to me.

Au Clair de la Lune

French Folksong

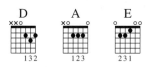

Strum Pattern: 4
Pick Pattern: 5

Verse
Slowly

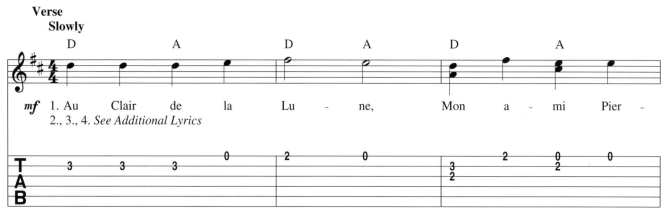

mf 1. Au Clair de la Lu - ne, Mon a - mi Pier -
2., 3., 4. *See Additional Lyrics*

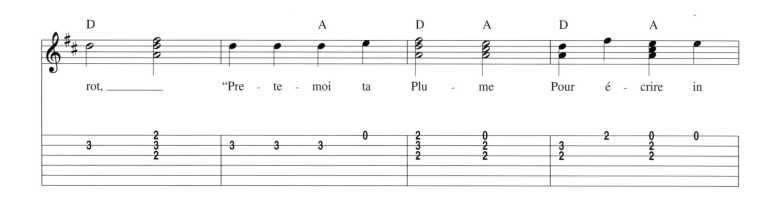

rot, _____ "Pre - te - moi ta Plu - me Pour é - crire in

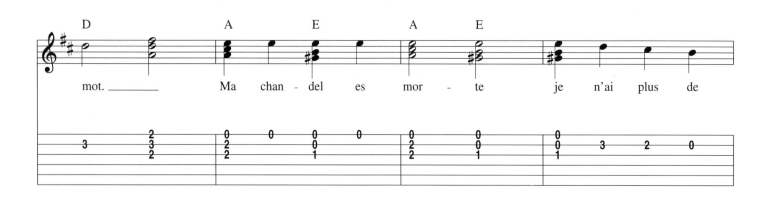

mot. _____ Ma chan - del es mor - te je n'ai plus de

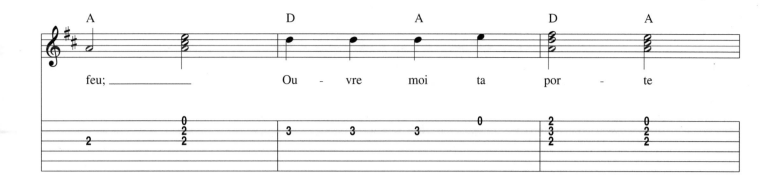

feu; _____ Ou - vre moi ta por - te

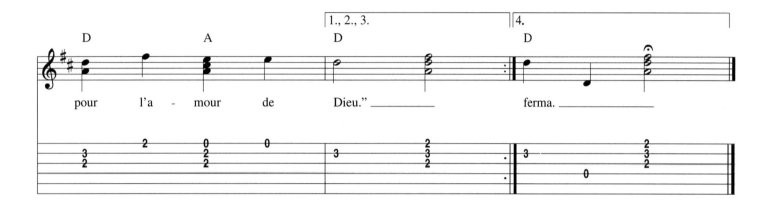

pour l'a - mour de Dieu." _____ ferma. _____

Additional Lyrics

2. Au Clair de la Lune Pierrot repondit,
   "Je n'ai pas de plume, je suis dans mon lit.
   Va chez la voisine, je crois qu'elle y est.
   Car dans sa cuisine on bat le briquet."

3. Au Clair de la Lune s'en fut Arlequin,
   Frapper chez la brune, ell' repond soudain:
   "Qui frapp' de la sorte?" Il dit a son tour:
   "Ouvrez vorte porte, pour le dieu d'amour!"

4. Au Clair de la Lune, on n'y voit qu'un peu.
   On chercha la plume, on chercha du fue.
   En cerchant d'la sorte, je n'sais c'qu'on trouva:
   Mais je sais qu'la porte sur eux se ferma.

English Lyrics

1. At the door I'm knocking, by the pale moonlight,
   "Lend me a pen, I pray thee, I've a word to write;
   Guttered is my candle, my fire burns no more;
   For the love of heaven, open up the door!"

2. Pierrot cried in answer by the pale moonlight,
   "In my bed I'm lying, late and chill the night;
   Yonder at my neighbor's someone is astir;
   Fire is freshly kindled, get a light from her."

3. To the neighbor's house then, by the pale moonlight,
   Goes our gentle Lubin to beg a pen to write;
   "Who knocks there so softly?" calls a voice above.
   "Open wide your door now for the God of Love!"

4. Seek thy pen and candle by the pale moonlight,
   They can see so little since dark is now the night;
   What they find while seeking, that is not revealed;
   All behind her door is carefully concealed.

Auld Lang Syne

Words by Robert Burns
Traditional Melody

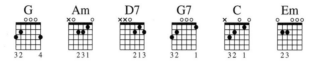

Strum Pattern: 3, 4
Pick Pattern: 2, 4

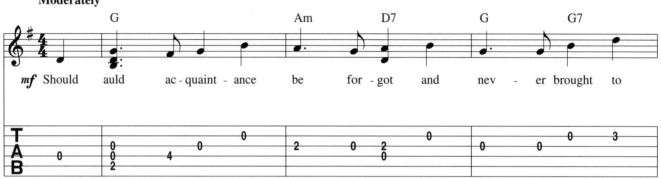

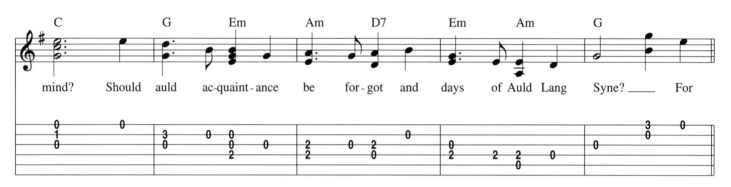

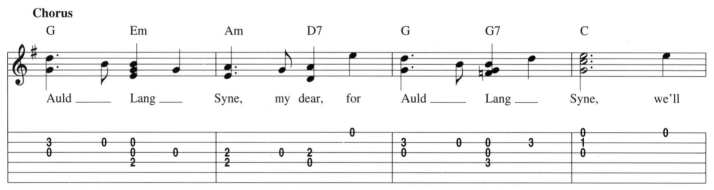

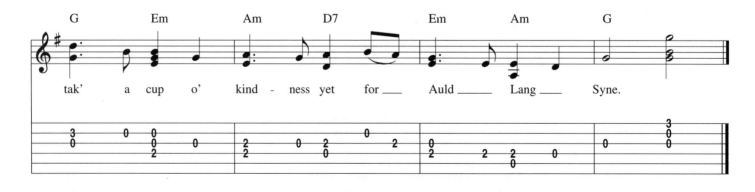

Carnival of Venice

Traditional

Strum Pattern: 7, 8
Pick Pattern: 8

Ay! Linda Amiga

Traditional

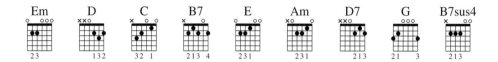

Strum Pattern: 3, 4
Pick Pattern: 3, 4

Verse
Moderately

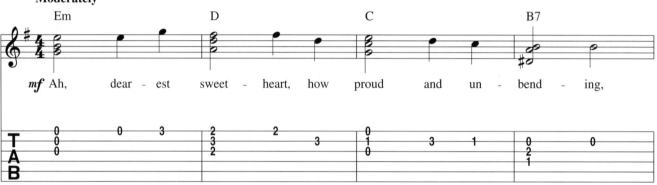

mf Ah, dear - est sweet - heart, how proud and un - bend - ing,

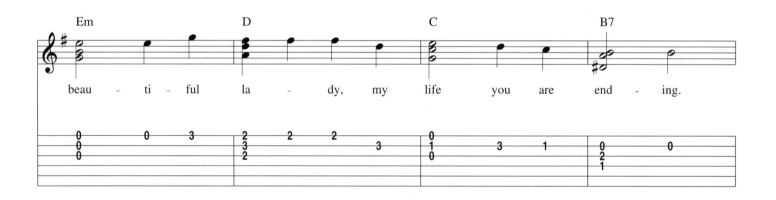

beau - ti - ful la - dy, my life you are end - ing.

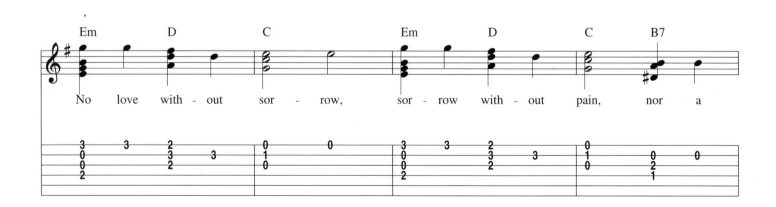

No love with - out sor - row, sor - row with - out pain, nor a

Ay! Linda amiga, que no vuelvoa verte
Cuerpo garrido, que me lleva a la muerte.
No hay amor sin pena, pena sin dolor,
Ni dolor tan agudo Como el del amor
Ni dolor tan agudo Como el del amor
Ay! Linda amiga, que no vuelvoa verte,
Cuerpo garrido, que me lleva a la muerte.

On the Beautiful Blue Danube, Op. 314

Johann Strauss

Strum Pattern: 8
Pick Pattern: 8

Campbells Are Coming

Traditional

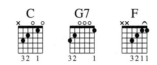

Strum Pattern: 8
Pick Pattern: 8

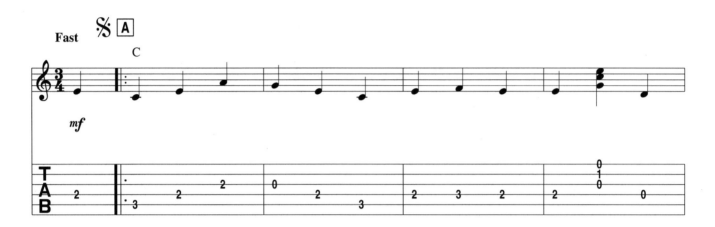

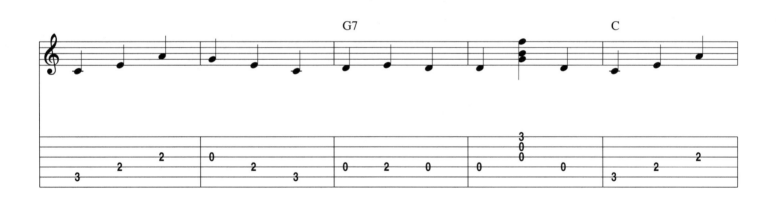

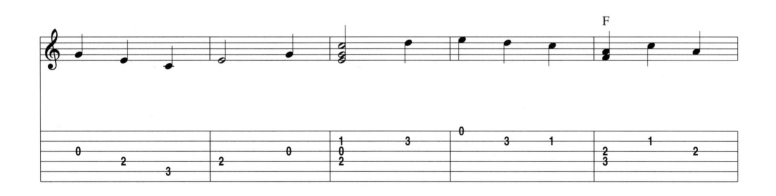

Chiapanecas

Traditional

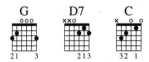

Strum Pattern: 8
Pick Pattern: 8

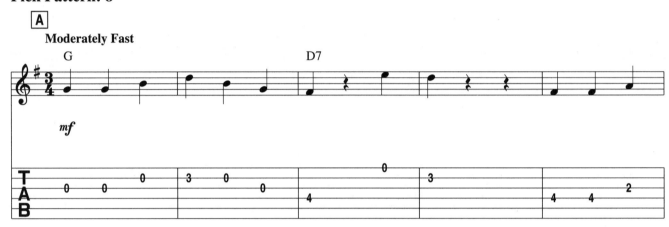

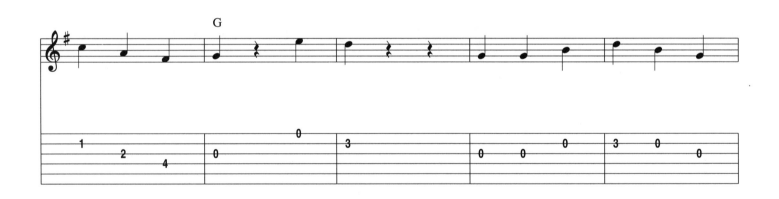

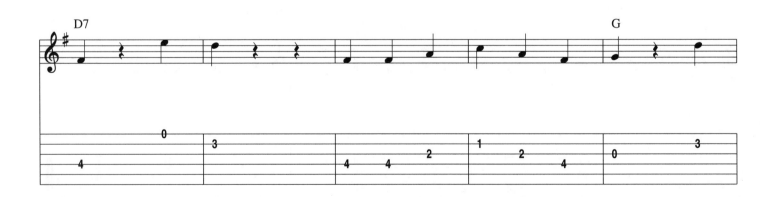

Cielito Lindo

Traditional

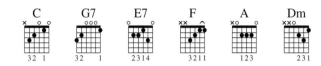

Strum Pattern: 8, 9
Pick Pattern: 8, 9

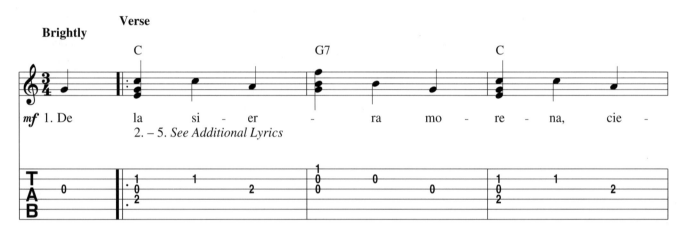

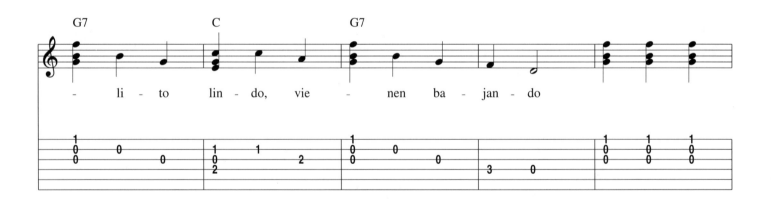

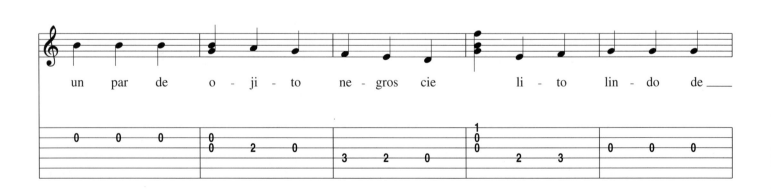

Additional Lyrics

2. Una flecha en el aire
   Cielito Lindo
   Lanzo Cupido
   Y como fue jugando,
   Y fui el herdo

3. Ese lunar que tienes
   Cielito Lindo
   Junto a la boca,
   Cielito Lindo,
   No se lo des a nadie
   Que a mi me toca

4. Pajaro que abandona
   Cielito Lindo
   Su primer nido,
   Vuelve y lo halla ocupando
   Cielito Lindo
   Y muy merecido.

5. Todas las ilucicnes
   Cielito Lindo
   Que el amor fragua,
   Son com las espunas
   Cielito Lindo
   Que forma el agua.

Chorus 5. Ay, ay, ay ay!
   Suben y crecen
   Y con el mismo viento
   Cielito Lindo,
   Desaparecen.

Come Back to Sorrento

Traditional

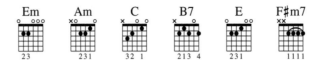

Strum Pattern: 7, 9
Pick Pattern: 8, 9

Intro
Moderately

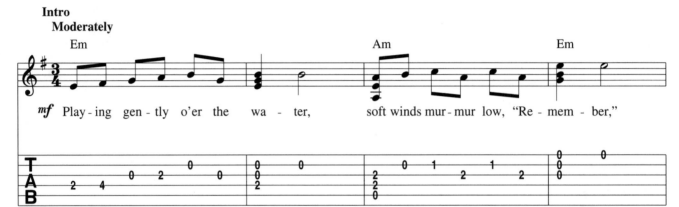

Play-ing gen-tly o'er the wa-ter, soft winds mur-mur low, "Re-mem-ber,"

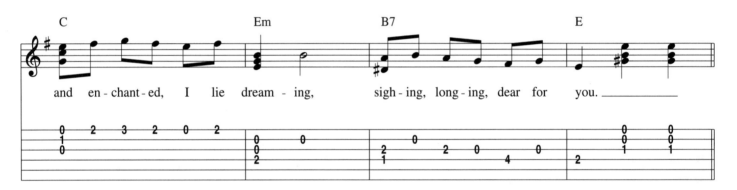

and en-chant-ed, I lie dream-ing, sigh-ing, long-ing, dear for you. _____

Verse

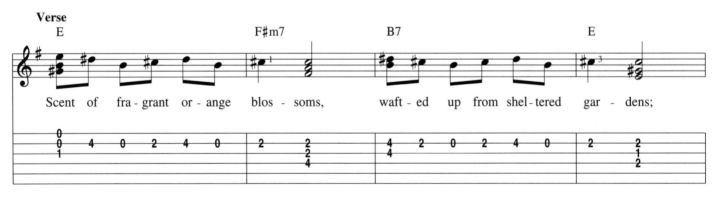

Scent of fra-grant or-ange blos-soms, waft-ed up from shel-tered gar-dens;

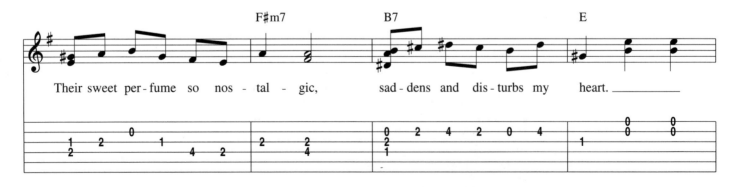

Their sweet per-fume so nos-tal-gic, sad-dens and dis-turbs my heart. _____

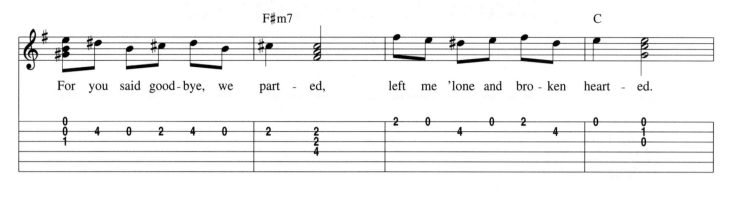

For you said good-bye, we part-ed, left me 'lone and bro-ken heart-ed.

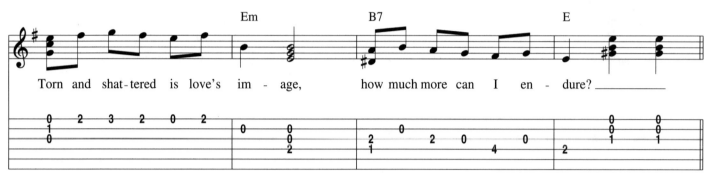

Torn and shat-tered is love's im-age, how much more can I en-dure? _____

Outro

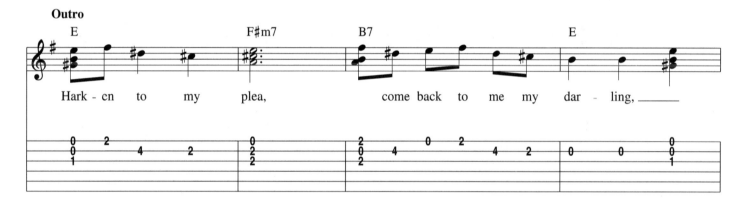

Hark-en to my plea, come back to me my dar-ling, _____

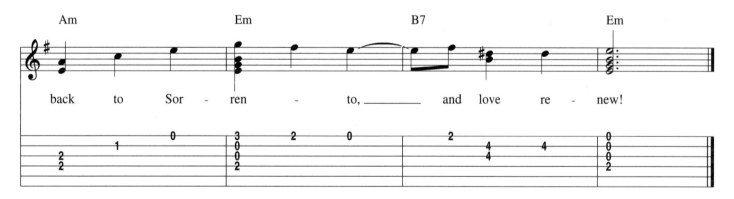

back to Sor-ren-to, _____ and love re-new!

Italian Lyrics

Guardail mare comé bello, spira tauto sentimento,
Come tuo soave accento cheme desto, fa sognar.
Senti come lieve sale dei giardini odor daranci;
Un profumo non v'haeguale per chi palpita d'a mor!
E tu dici "Io parto addio!"
T'allontani dal mio core; questa terra dell' a more
Hai la forza di lasciar?
Ma non mi fugir, non darmi piu' tormento,
Torna a Surriento, non farmi morir!

Comin' Through the Rye

Traditional

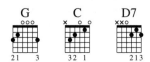

Strum Pattern: 9
Pick Pattern: 8, 9

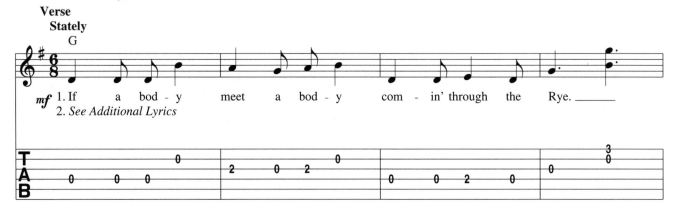

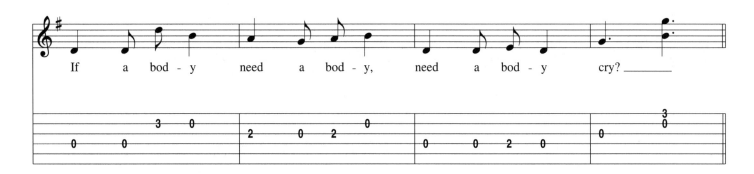

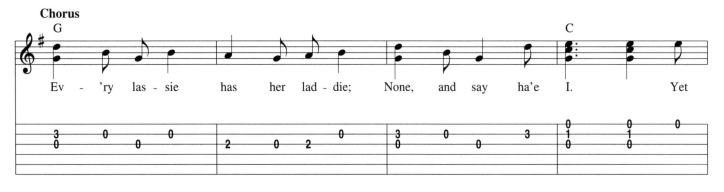

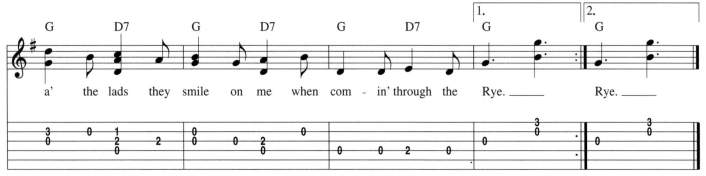

Additional Lyrics

2. If a body meet a body comin' frae the town.
   If a body greet a body, need a body frown?

Dark Eyes

Traditional

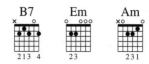

Strum Pattern: 7
Pick Pattern: 8

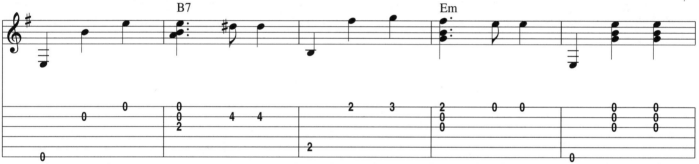

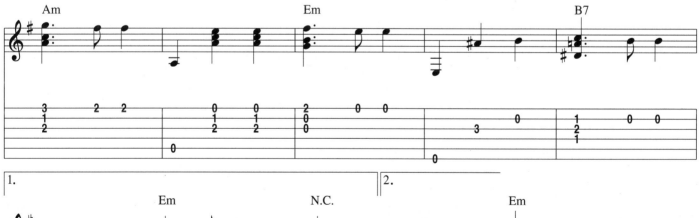

Danny Boy (Londonderry Air)

Words by Frederick Edward Weatherly
Music is Irish Traditional

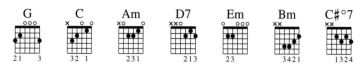

Strum Pattern: 4
Pick Pattern: 4

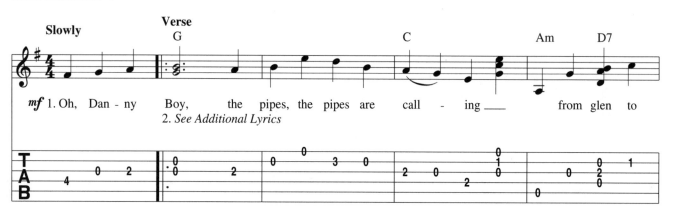

Slowly

mf 1. Oh, Dan - ny Boy, the pipes, the pipes are call - ing ___ from glen to
2. *See Additional Lyrics*

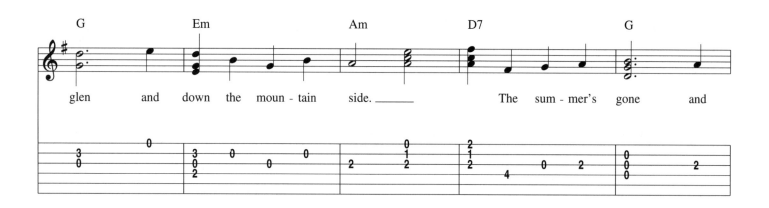

glen and down the moun - tain side. ___ The sum - mer's gone and

all the ros - es fall - ing. ___ 'Tis you, 'tis you must go and I must

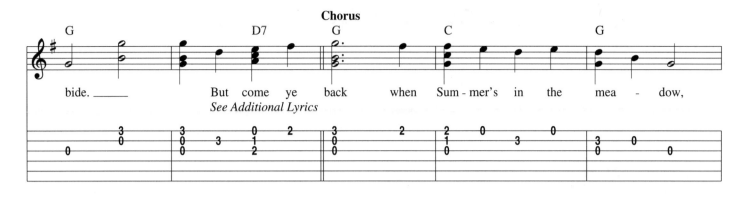

bide. _____   But come ye back   when   Sum - mer's   in   the   mea - dow,
See Additional Lyrics

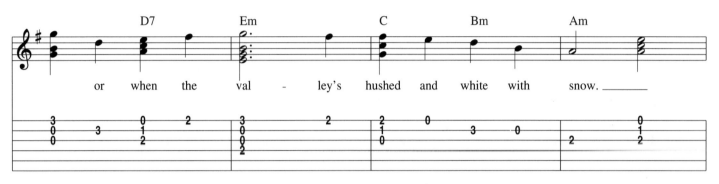

or   when   the   val - ley's   hushed   and   white   with   snow. _____

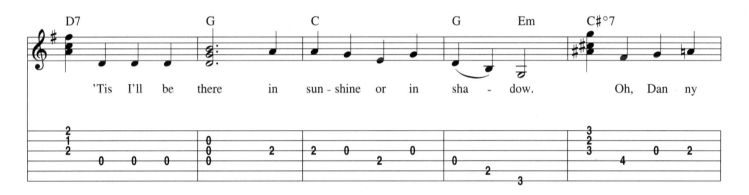

'Tis   I'll   be   there   in   sun - shine   or   in   sha - dow.   Oh,   Dan - ny

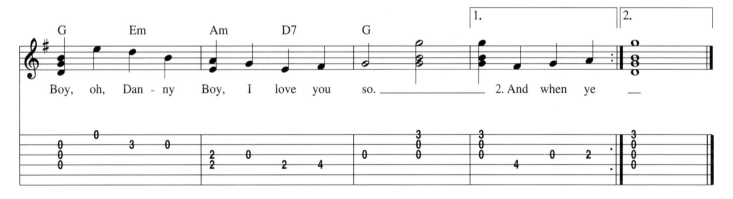

Boy,   oh,   Dan - ny   Boy,   I   love   you   so. _____   2. And   when   ye   __

Additional Lyrics

2. And when ye come and all the flowers are dying,
   If I am dead, and dead I well may be,
   You'll come and find the place where I am lying,
   And kneel and say an Ave there for me.

Chorus And I shall hear, tho' soft you tread above me.
   And all my grave will warmer, sweeter be.
   If you will bend and tell me that you love me
   Then I shall sleep in peace until you come to me.

Du Du Liegst Mir Im Herzen

Traditional

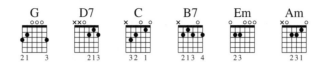

Strum Pattern: 7, 8
Pick Pattern: 8, 9

Verse
Bright Waltz

mf 1.You, you, in my heart liv - ing, you,
2., 3., 4. *See Additional Lyrics*

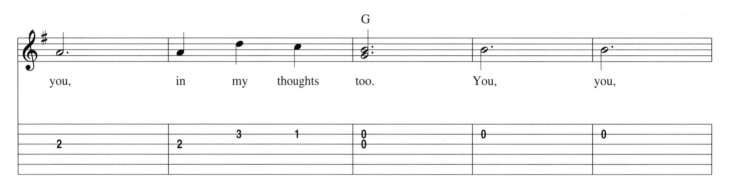

you, in my thoughts too. You, you,

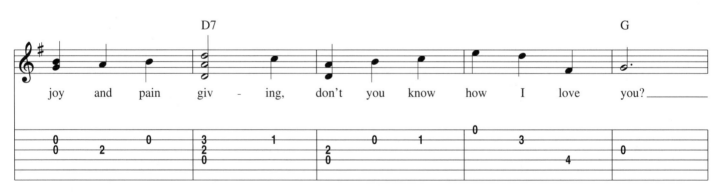

joy and pain giv - ing, don't you know how I love you?

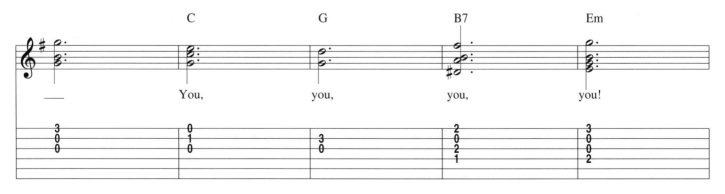

You, you, you, you!

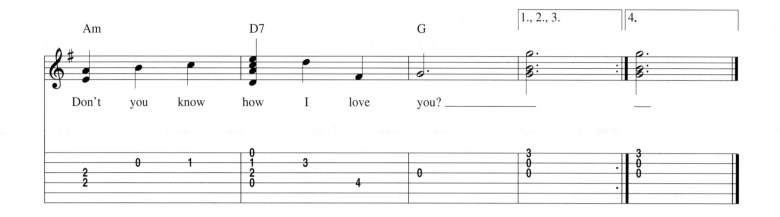

Don't you know how I love you? _____ _____

Additional Lyrics

2. You, you have my devotion.
   You, you give yours to me!
   Oh, oh, fondest emotion
   I feel for you tenderly.
   You, you, you, you!
   I feel for you tenderly.

3. Still, still won't you be showing
   Some, some sign you are true?
   Why not trust in me knowing
   How good I am, dear, to you!
   You, you, you, you!
   How good I am, dear, to you!

4. If in dreams someday clearly
   To you my face appears,
   Then, then, may love so dearly
   Unite us all through the years.
   Love, love, love, love,
   Unite us all through the years.

German Lyrics

1. Du, du liegst mir im Herzen
   Du, du liegst mir im sinn;
   Du, du machst mir viel schmerzen,
   Weisst nicht wie gut ich dir bin!
   Ja, ja, ja, ja,
   Weist nicht wie gut ich dir bin.

2. So, so wie ich dich liebe,
   So, so liebe auch mich!
   Die, die zartlichsten Triebe
   Fuhl ich allien nur fur dich.
   Ja, ja, ja, ja,
   Fuhl ich allien nur fur dich.

3. Doch, doch, darf ich dir trauen,
   Dir, dir mit leichtem Sinn?
   Du, du darfst auf mich bauen,
   Ja, ja, ja, ja,
   Weist ja, wie gut ich dir bin!. . .

4. Und, und, wenn in der Ferne,
   Dir, dir mein Bild erscheint,
   Dann, dann wunscht ich so gerne,
   Lieb', lieb', lieb', lieb',
   Dass uns die Liebe vereint!. . .

Funiculi, Funicula

Traditional

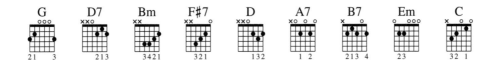

Strum Pattern: 7
Pick Pattern: 7

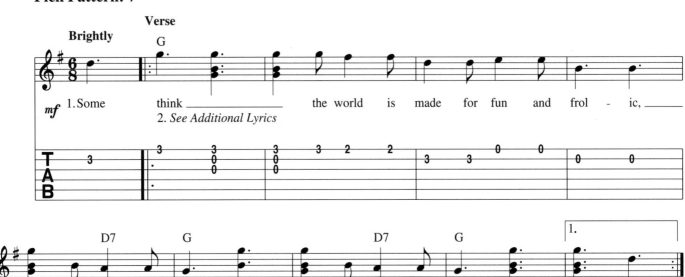

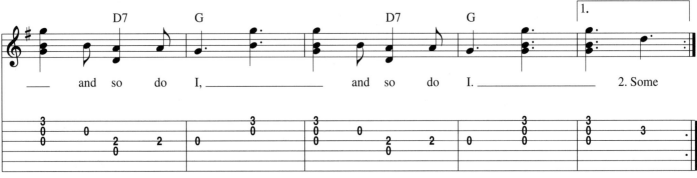

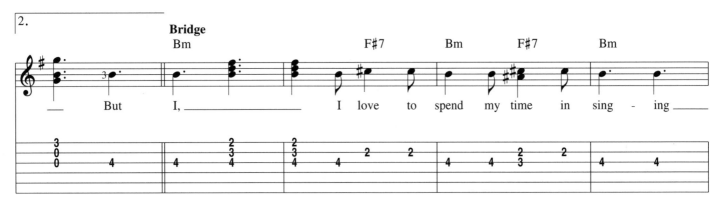

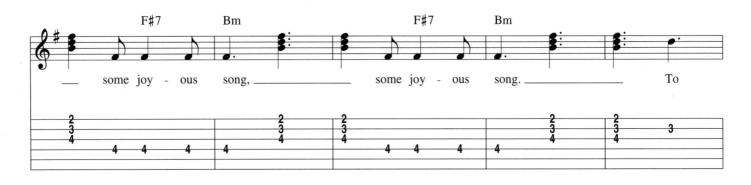

Additional Lyrics

2. Some think it well to be all melancholic,
To pine and sigh, to pine and sigh.

Greensleeves

Traditional English

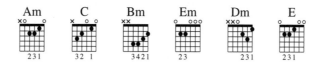

Strum Pattern: 7
Pick Pattern: 7

Verse
Slowly

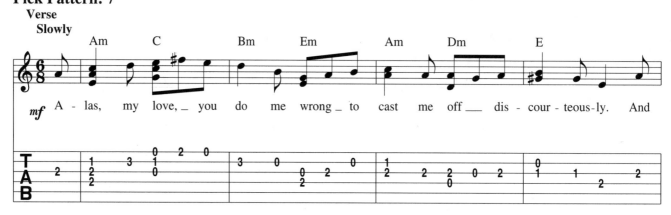

A - las, my love, _ you do me wrong _ to cast me off _ dis - cour - teous - ly. And

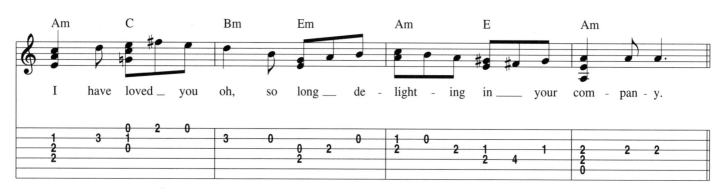

I have loved _ you oh, so long _ de - light - ing in _ your com - pan - y.

Chorus

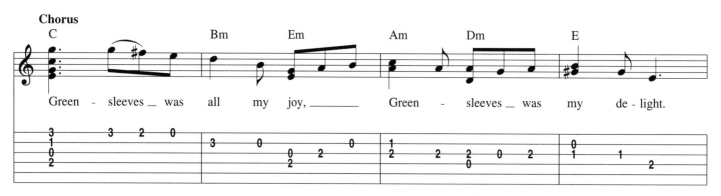

Green - sleeves _ was all my joy, _____ Green - sleeves _ was my de - light.

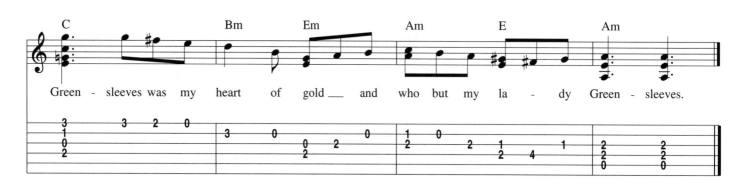

Green - sleeves was my heart of gold _ and who but my la - dy Green - sleeves.

John Peel

Traditional

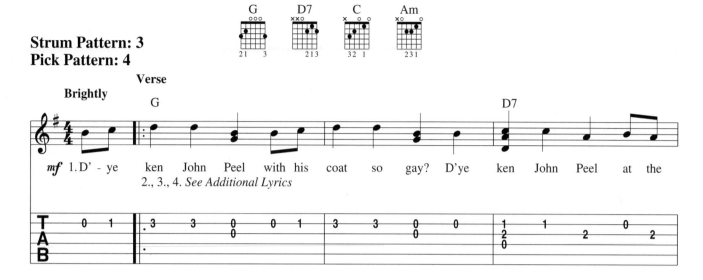

Strum Pattern: 3
Pick Pattern: 4

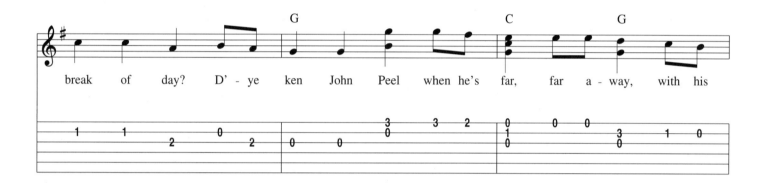

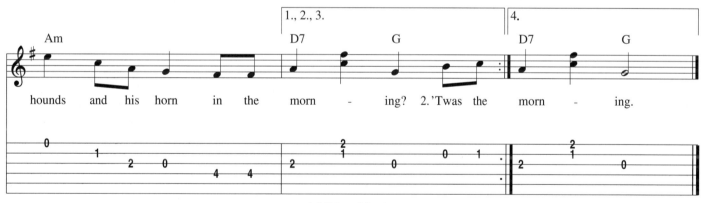

Additional Lyrics

2. 'Twas the sound of his horn brought me from my bed,
   And the cry of his hounds which he oft' times led,
   For Peel's "View Hallo!" would awaken the dead,
   Or the fox from his lair in the morning.

3. Yes, I ken John Peel and Ruby too!
   Rauter and Ringwood, Bellman and True.
   From a find to a check, from a check to a view,
   With a view to a death in the morning.

4. D'ye ken John Peel with his coat so gay?
   He lived at Troutbeck once on a day,
   Now he has gone far, far away,
   We shall ne'er hear his voice in the morning.

Hava Nagilah

Traditional

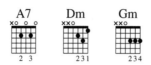

Strum Pattern: 4
Pick Pattern: 4

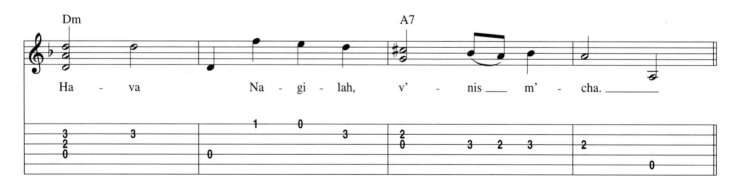

Kum Ba Yah

Traditional

Strum Pattern: 4
Pick Pattern: 1, 2

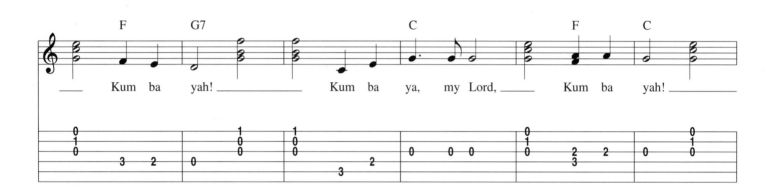

Additional Lyrics

2. Hear me crying, Lord, Kum ba ya!
   Hear me crying, Lord, Kum ba ya!
   Hear me crying, Lord, Kum ba ya!
   Oh Lord! Kum ba ya!

3. Hear me praying, Lord, Kum ba ya!
   Hear me praying, Lord, Kum ba ya!
   Hear me praying, Lord, Kum ba ya!
   O Lord! Kum ba ya!

4. Oh I need you, Lord, Kum ba ya!
   Oh I need you, Lord, Kum ba ya!
   Oh I need you, Lord, Kum ba ya!
   Oh Lord! Kum ba ya!

La Donna è Mobile

By G. Verdi

Strum Pattern: 8
Pick Pattern: 8

Verse
Brightly

1. La Don - na è Mo - bi - le qual piu ma ven - to
2. *See Additional Lyrics*

mu - ta - d'ac - cen - to e di pen - sie - ro.

Chorus

La - Don - na è mo - bil qual ___ piu ma al

ven - to ___ mu - ta d'ac - cen - to e ___ di pen - sier.

Additional Lyrics

2. Sempre un a Mobile qual piu ma al vento
   Mu ta d'accento e di pensiero.

La Cucaracha

Traditional

Strum Pattern: 3
Pick Pattern: 4

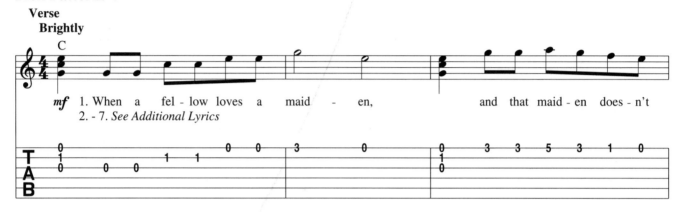

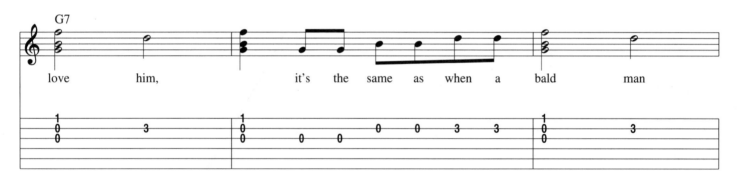

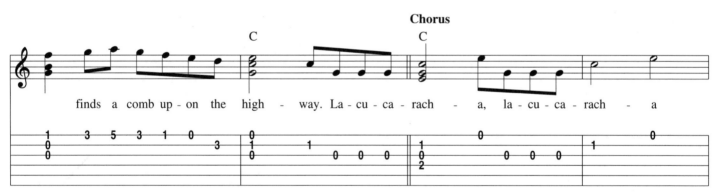

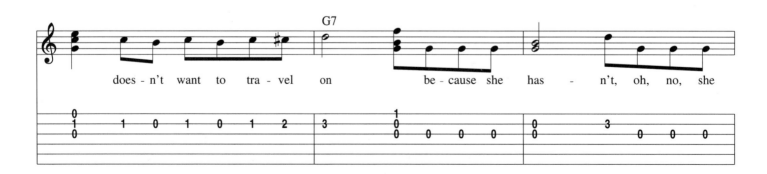

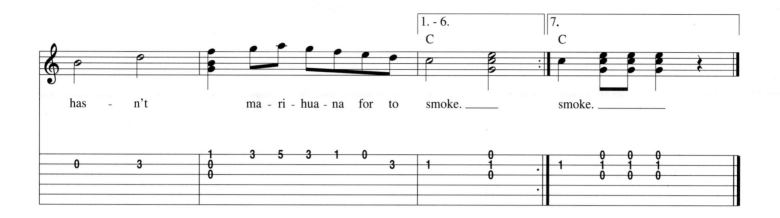

has - n't   ma - ri - hua - na for to smoke. _____   smoke. _____

Additional Lyrics

2. All the maidens are of pure gold;
   All the married girls are silver;
   All the widows are of copper,
   And old women merely tin.

3. My neighbor across the highway
   Used to be called Dona Clara,
   And if she has not expired
   Likely that's her name tomorrow.

4. All the girls up at Las Vegas
   Are most awful tall and skinny,
   But they're worse for plaintive pleading
   Than the souls of Purgatory.

5. All the girls here in the city
   Don't know how to give you kisses,
   While the ones from Albuquerque
   Stretch their necks to avoid misses.

6. All the girls from Mexico
   Are as pretty as a flower
   And they talk so very sweetly,
   Fill your heart quite up with love.

7. One thing makes me laugh most hearty
   Pancho Villa with no shirt on
   Now the Carranzistas beat it
   Because Villa's men are coming.

Spanish Lyrics

1. Cuando uno quiera a una,
   Ycsta una nolo quiera,
   Es lo mismo que si un calvo
   En la calle encuen trún peine.

   Chorus:
   La cucaracha, la cucaracha
   Ya no quieras cominar,
   Porque no tienes, porque la falta
   Marihuana que fumar.

2. Las muchachas son de orro;
   Las casadas son de plata;
   Las viudas son de cobre,
   Y las viejas oja de lata.

3. Mi vecina de enfrente
   Se llamaba Dona Clara
   Y si no habia muerto
   Es probable se llamara.

4. Las muchachas de La Vegas
   Son muy altas y delgaditas
   Pero son mas pediguenas
   Que las animas benditas.

5. Las muchachas de la villa
   No saben ni dar un beso.
   Cuando las de Albuquerque
   Hasta estiran el pescuezo.

6. Las muchachas Mexicanas
   Son lindas como un flor,
   Y hablan tan dulcemente
   Que encantan de amor.

7. Una cosa me da risa
   Pancho Villa sin vamisa.
   Ya se van los Carranzistas
   Porque vienen los Villistas.

Loch Lomand

Traditional

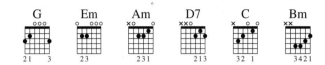

Strum Pattern: 3
Pick Pattern: 4

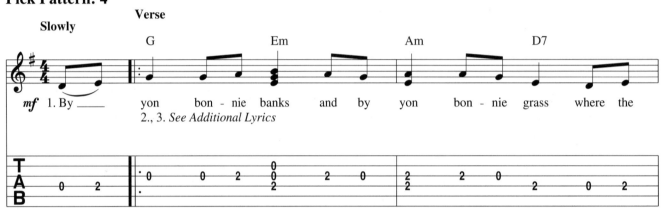

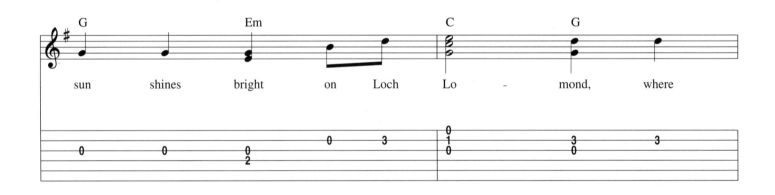

bon - nie, bon - nie banks   of   Loch   Lo -   mond.   Oh!   Y'ell   take   the   high   road, and

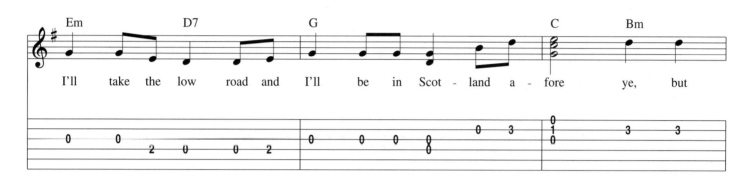

I'll   take   the   low   road   and   I'll   be   in   Scot - land   a - fore   ye,   but

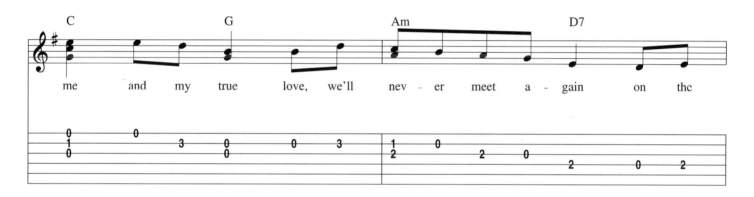

me   and   my   true   love,   we'll   nev - er   meet   a - gain   on   the

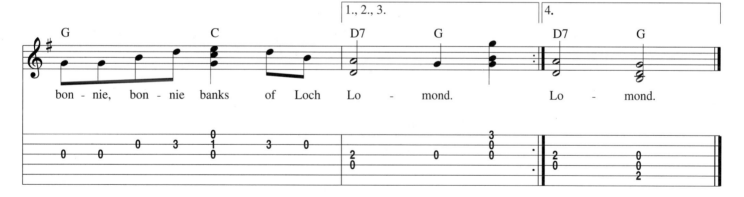

bon - nie, bon - nie   banks   of   Loch   Lo -   mond.   Lo -   mond.

Additional Lyrics

2. 'Twas then that we parted in yon shady glen,
On the steep, steep side of Ben Lomond.
Where in purple hue, the Highland hills we view
And the moon coming out in the gloaming.

3. The wee birdies sing, and the wildflowers spring,
And in sunshine, the waters are sleeping.
But the broken heart, it kens, nae second spring again,
Tho' the woeful may cease their greeting.

Marianne

Traditional

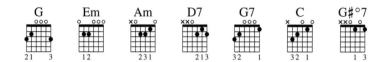

Strum Pattern: 2
Pick Pattern: 3, 4

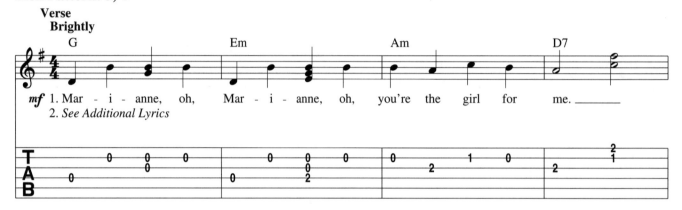

Verse
Brightly

mf 1. Mar - i - anne, oh, Mar - i - anne, oh, you're the girl for me. ____
2. *See Additional Lyrics*

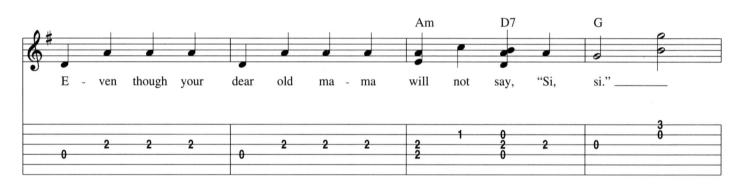

E - ven though your dear old ma - ma will not say, "Si, si." ____

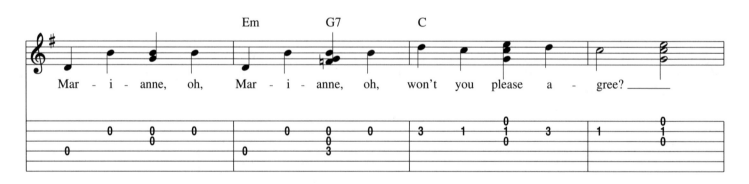

Mar - i - anne, oh, Mar - i - anne, oh, won't you please a - gree? ____

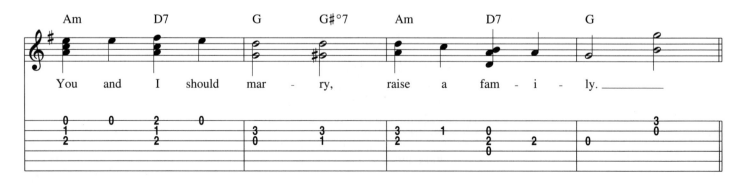

You and I should mar - ry, raise a fam - i - ly. ____

Chorus

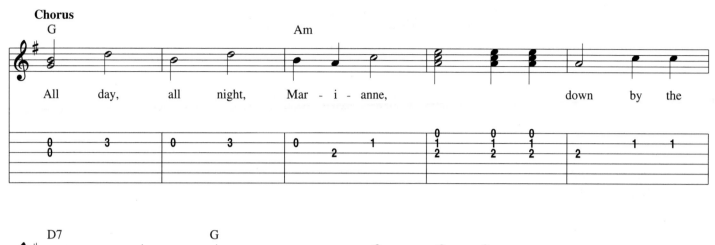

All day, all night, Mar - i - anne, down by the

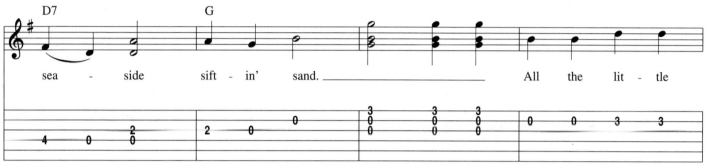

sea - side sift - in' sand. _____ All the lit - tle

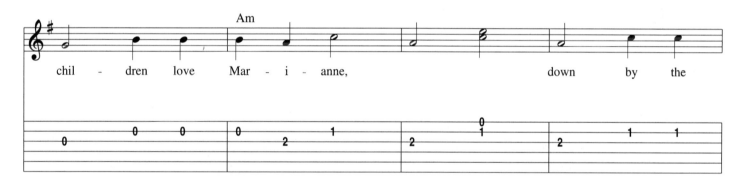

chil - dren love Mar - i - anne, down by the

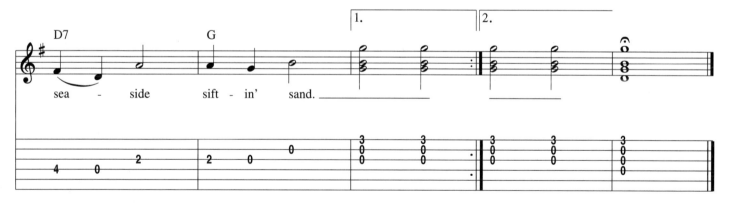

sea - side sift - in' sand. _____

Additional Lyrics

2. When I met sweet Marianne,
   Her mother said to me:
   "Where do you stand financially?"
   She does not approve of me,
   'Cause I'm no millionaire,
   But I love her daughter,
   More than I can bear.

Mexican Hat Dance

Traditional

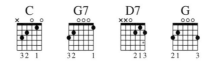

Strum Pattern: 7, 8
Pick Pattern: 8

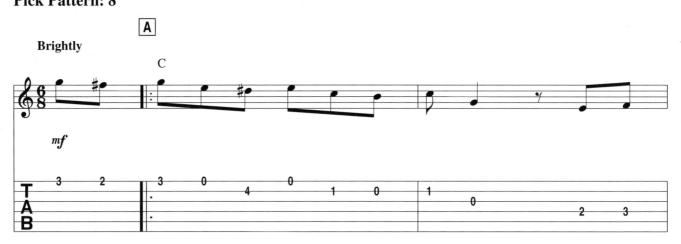

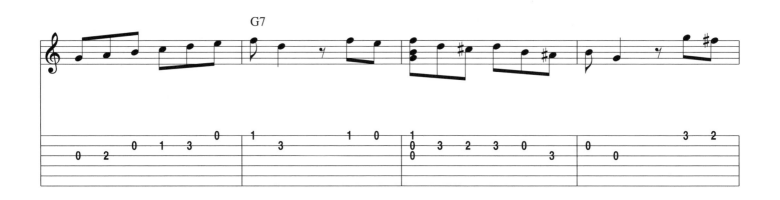

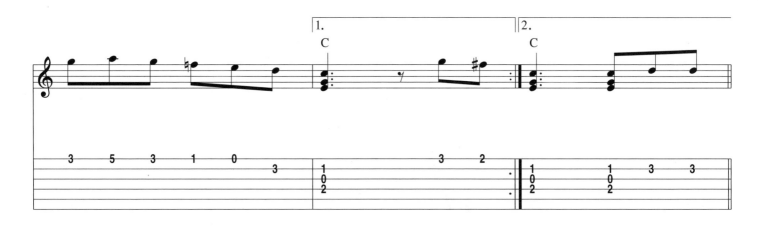

Molly Malone (Cockles & Mussels)

Traditional

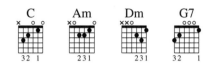

Strum Pattern: 7, 8
Pick Pattern: 9

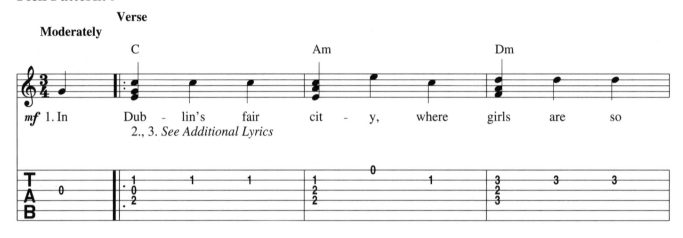

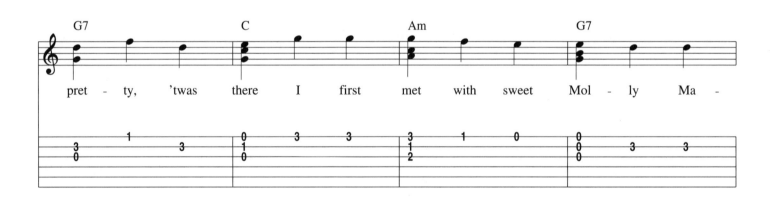

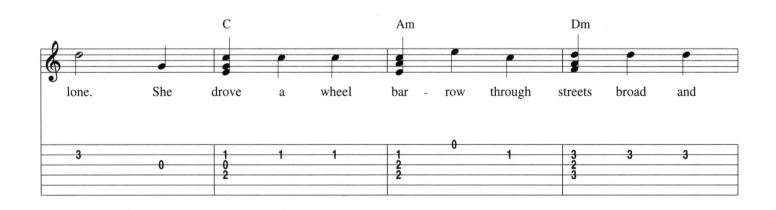

Additional Lyrics

2. She was a fish monger, but sure was no wonder,
   For so were her mother and father before.
   They drove their wheel barrows
   Through streets broad and narrow
   Crying, "Cockles and mussels, alive, alive-o.
   Alive, alive-o, alive, alive-o,"
   Crying, "Cockles and mussels, alive, alive-o."

3. She died of a fever, and nothing could save her,
   And that was the end of sweet Molly Malone.
   Her ghost wheels a barrow
   Through streets broad and narrow,
   Crying, "Cockles and mussels, alive, alive-o.
   Alive, alive-o, alive, alive-o,"
   Crying, "Cockles and mussels, alive, alive-o."

My Bonnie

Traditional

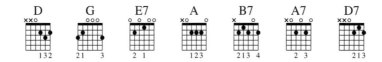

Strum Pattern: 7, 8
Pick Pattern: 8, 9

Verse
Moderately

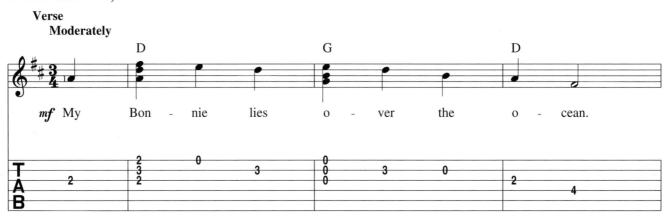

My Bon – nie lies o – ver the o – cean.

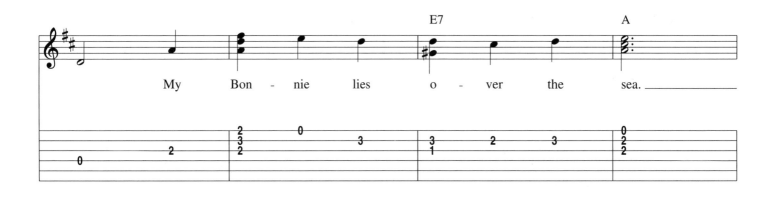

My Bon – nie lies o – ver the sea. ____

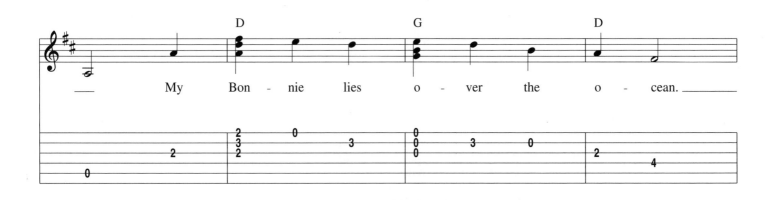

____ My Bon – nie lies o – ver the o – cean.

My Wild Irish Rose

Words and Music by Chauncey Olcott

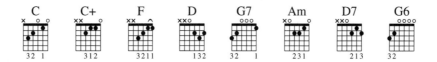

Strum Pattern: 7, 9
Pick Pattern: 8

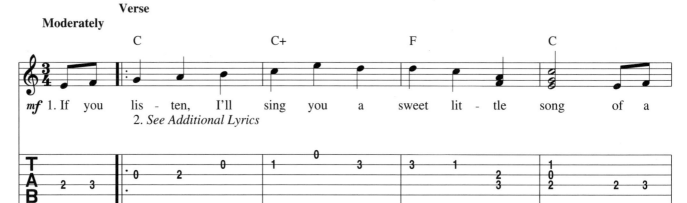

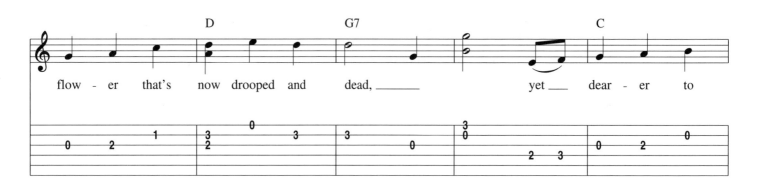

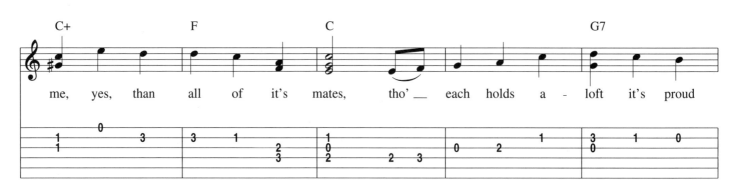

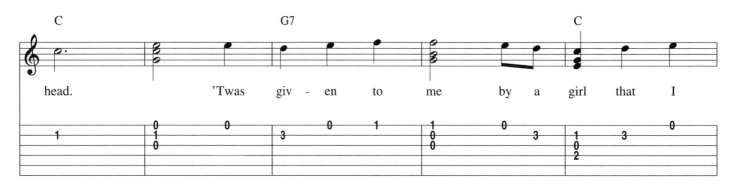

50

Additional Lyrics

2. They may sing of their roses, which by other names,
   Would smell just as sweetly, they say,
   But I know that my rose would never consent
   To have that sweet name taken away.
   Her glances are shy when e'er I pass by
   The bower where my true love grows.

Plaisir d'amour

By Giovanni Martini

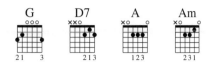

Strum Pattern: 9
Pick Pattern: 9

Verse
Moderately

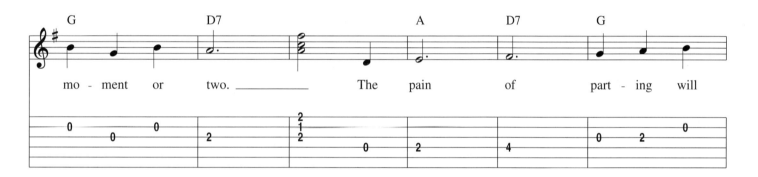

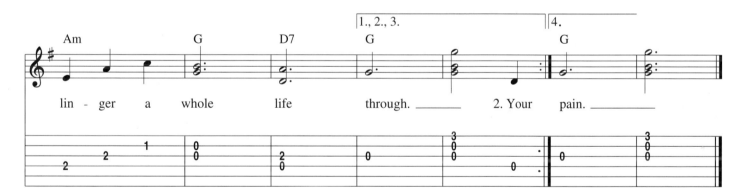

Additional Lyrics

2. Your love for me seemed oh so perfect and true,
   Yet here I am, in my sadness, rememb'ring you.

3. The skies were fair when I could call you my own,
   And now the fair skies have vanished and I'm all alone.

4. A fool was I to think your love would remain,
   Oh yes, your love had its pleasure, but more of pain.

'O Sole Mio

Words by Giovanni Capurro
Music by Edorado di Capua

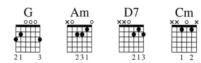

Strum Pattern: 3, 6
Pick Pattern: 2

Verse
Moderately

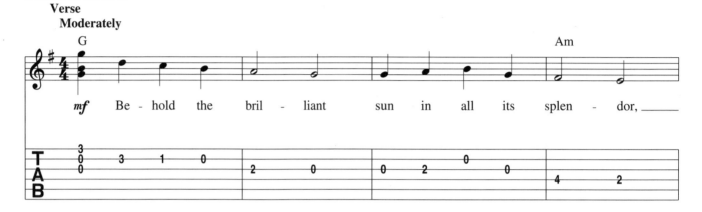

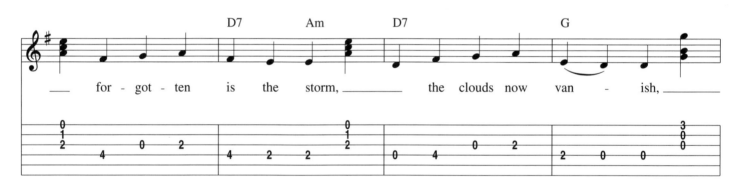

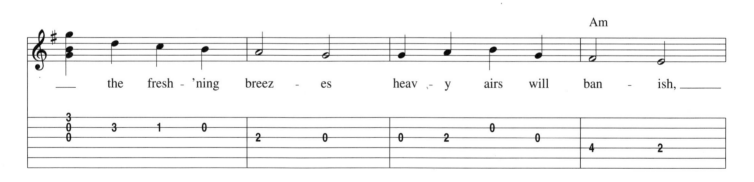

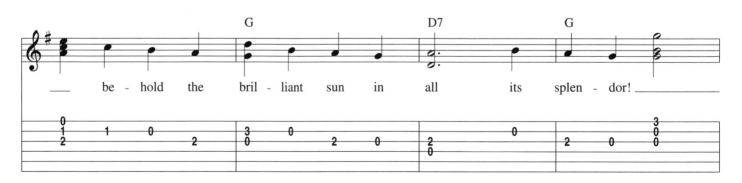

Chorus

Sakura

Traditional Japanese Folk Song

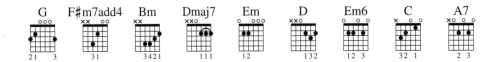

Strum Pattern: 3, 4
Pick Pattern: 2, 4

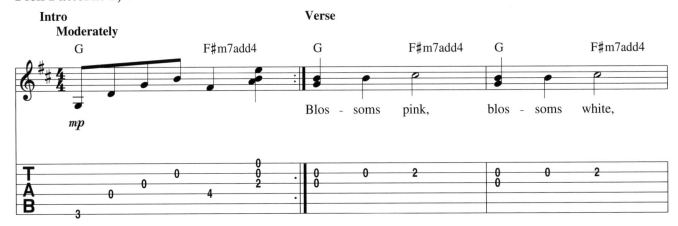

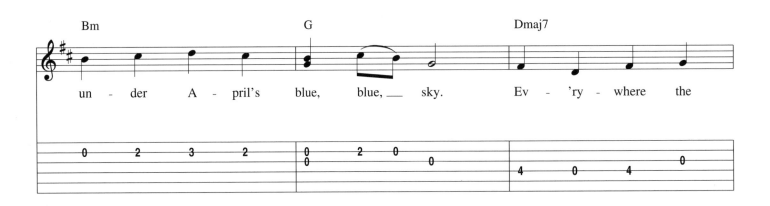

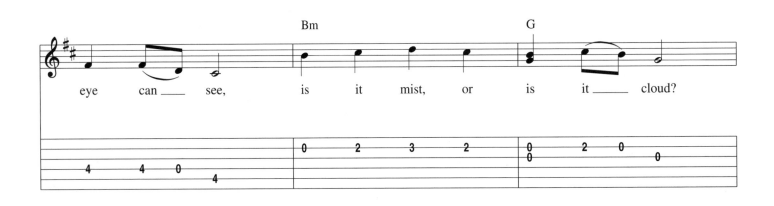

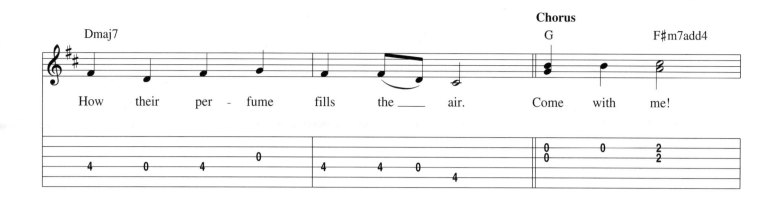

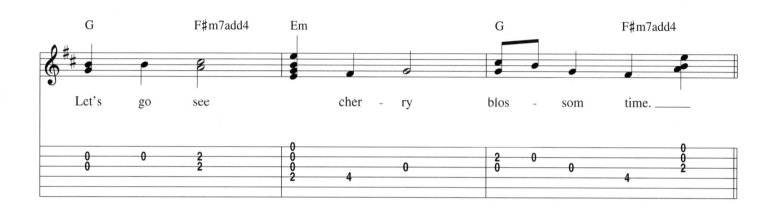

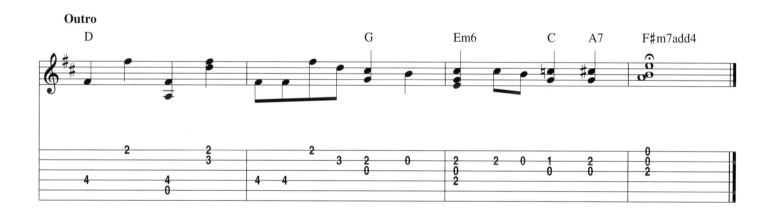

Japanese Lyrics

Verse   Sakura! Sakura!
Yayoi no sora wa,
Miwatasu kagiri, kasumi ka? Kumo ka?
Nioi zo izu ru.

Chorus   Izaya! Izaya!
Mini yukan.

Toom Balalaika

Traditional

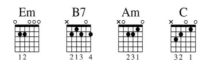

Strum Pattern: 8, 9
Pick Pattern: 7, 8

Verse
Moderately

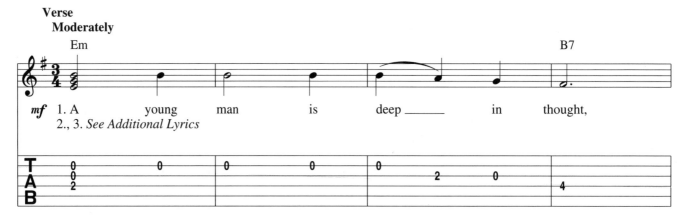

1. A young man is deep _____ in thought,
2., 3. *See Additional Lyrics*

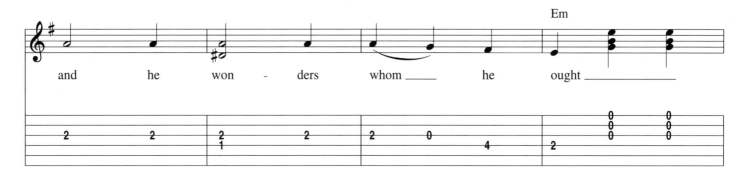

and he won - ders whom _____ he ought _____

to take as wife for all of his life, to

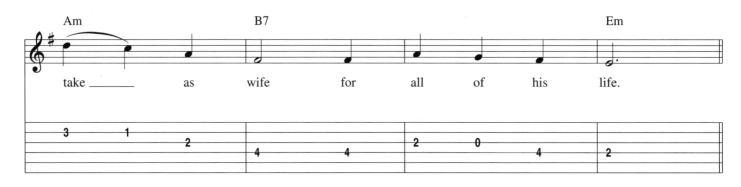

take _____ as wife for all of his life.

Chorus

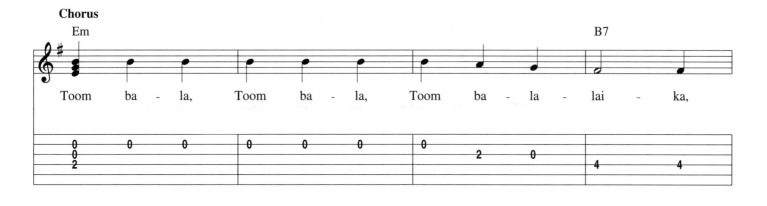

Toom ba - la, Toom ba - la, Toom ba - la - lai - ka,

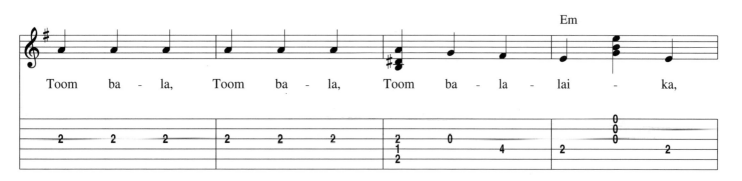

Toom ba - la, Toom ba - la, Toom ba - la - lai - ka,

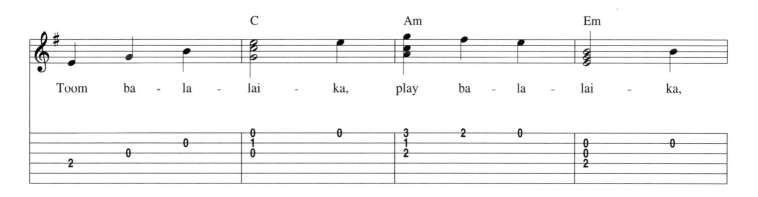

Toom ba - la - lai - ka, play ba - la - lai - ka,

play ba - la - lai - ka, let there be joy. joy.

Additional Lyrics

2. Tell me, maiden, I'd like to know,
   What it is needs no rain to grow?
   What's not consumed though it's burning?
   What weeps no tears although it's yearning.

3. You foolish boy, didn't you know,
   A stone does not need rain to grow,
   A love's not consumed although it's burning,
   A heart weeps no tears although it's yearning.

Volga Boat Song

Traditional

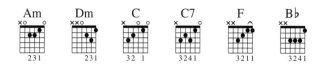

Strum Pattern: 3, 4
Pick Pattern: 3, 4

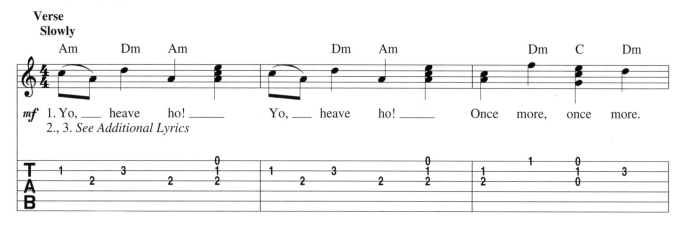

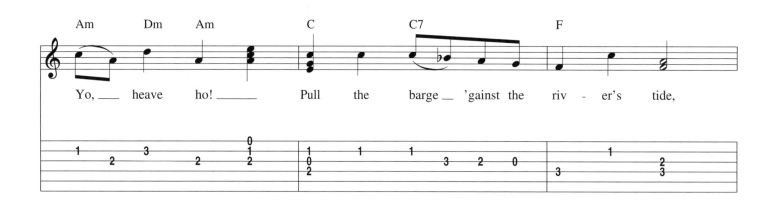

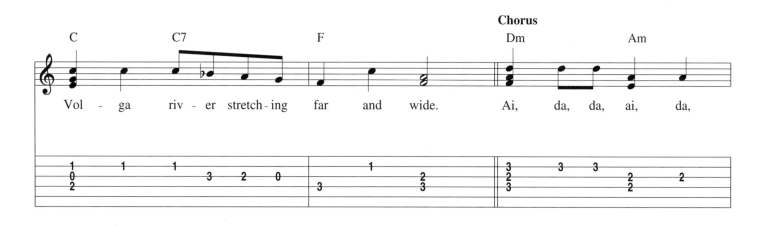

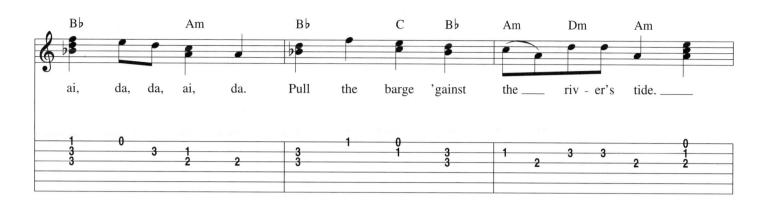

ai, da, da, ai, da. Pull the barge 'gainst the ___ riv - er's tide. ___

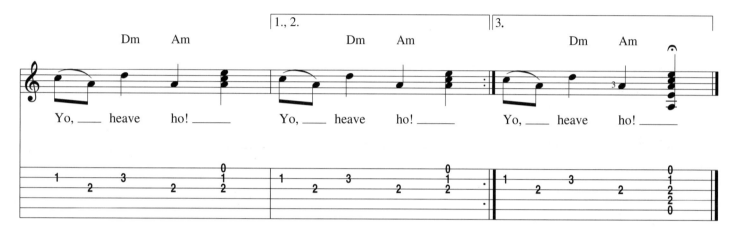

1., 2.

Yo, ___ heave ho! ___ Yo, ___ heave ho! ___

3.

Yo, ___ heave ho! ___

Additional Lyrics

2. Yo, heave ho! Yo, heave ho!
   Once more, once more. Yo, heave ho!
   As the barges float along,
   To the sun we sing our song…

3. Yo, heave ho! Yo, heave ho!
   Once more, once more. Yo, heave ho!
   Volga, Volga our pride,
   Mighty stream so deep and wide.

When Irish Eyes Are Smiling

Words by Chauncey Olcott and George Graff, Jr.
Music by Ernest R. Ball

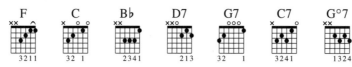

Strum Pattern: 7, 9
Pick Pattern: 8

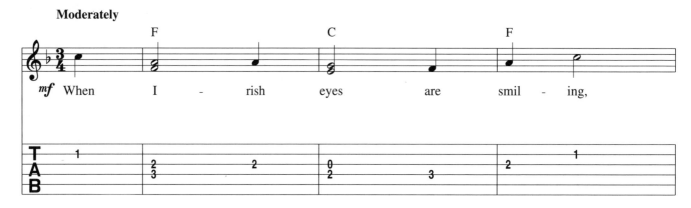

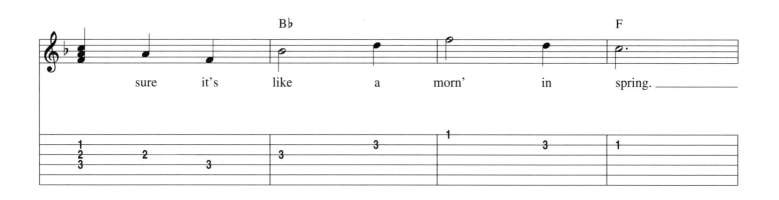

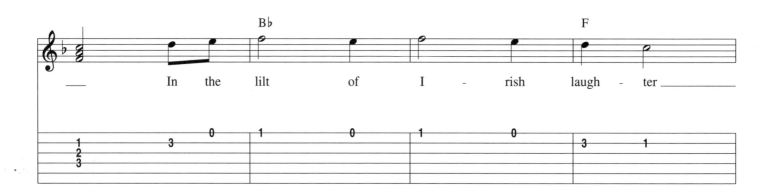

Santa Lucia

Traditional

Strum Pattern: 8, 9
Pick Pattern: 8, 9

Verse
Slowly

mf 1. Now 'neath the sil-ver moon, o-cean is glow-ing. O'er the calm bil-lows,
2., 3., 4. *See Additional Lyrics*

Chorus

soft winds are blow-ing. Hark, how the sail-ors cry, joy-ous-ly ech-oes sigh,

To Coda

D.C. al Coda
(take repeat)

San-ta — Lu-ci-a, San-ta Lu-ci-a.

Coda

San-ta Lu-ci-a.

Additional Lyrics

2. Here balmy breezes blow, pure joys invite us.
And as we gently row, all things delight us.

3. When o'er the waters, light winds are playing;
Their spell can soothe us, all care allaying.

4. Thee, sweet Napoli, what charms are given.
Where smiles creation, toil blessed heaven.